International Food Library

FOOD IN
FRANCE

International Food Library

FOOD IN
FRANCE

text by
Nancy Loewen

recipes compiled by
Judith A. Ahlstrom

Rourke Publications, Inc.
Vero Beach, Florida 32964

Library of Congress Cataloging-in-Publication Data

Loewen, Nancy, 1964-
   Food in France / by Nancy Loewen
      p. cm. — (International food library)
   Includes index.
   Summary: Describes the dishes, food habits, and special festivals of France.
   ISBN 0-86625-344-0
   1. Cookery, French—Juvenile literature.   2. Food habits—France—Juvenile literature.   [1. Cookery, French.   2. Food habits—France.   3. France—Social life and customs.]   I. Title.
II. Series.
TX719.L63   1991
641.5944—dc20   90-42582
                                     CIP
                                     AC

CONTENTS

AN INTRODUCTION TO FRANCE

France is the second largest country in Europe, after the Soviet Union. It lies between the Atlantic Ocean and the Mediterranean Sea, and shares a border with many countries: Spain to the southwest; Italy, Switzerland, and Germany to the east; and Luxembourg and Belgium to the north. To the west is the Bay of Biscay, and to the northwest is the English Channel, both of which lead to the Atlantic Ocean. The Mediterranean Sea lies to the southeast.

With a population of more than 56 million, France is one of the most heavily populated countries in the world. Paris is the capital, and nearly one of every six people lives in the Paris metropolitan area. Three-

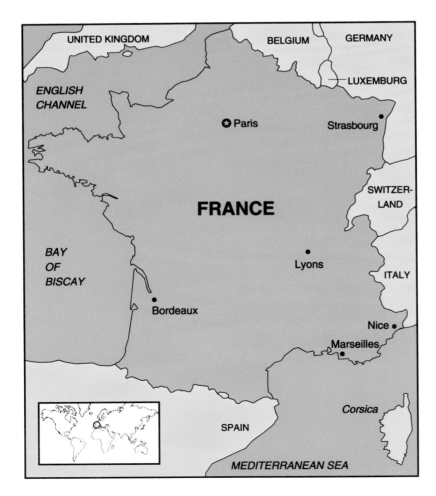

Paris is often called "The City of Lights." Near the center of the picture is the famous Eiffel Tower.

fourths of the people live in cities and towns of more than 2,000. Besides Paris, major cities include Marseilles, Lyons, Nice, Strasbourg, and Bordeaux.

The variations and contrasts in France are fascinating to people around the world. One of France's main attractions, of course, is the glamour and sophistication of Paris and other large cities. Here people can visit some of the world's finest museums and art galleries, stroll through famous parks, and dine at impossibly elegant restaurants. They can shop, go to concerts and plays, and perhaps get a glimpse of well-known models, actors, artists, writers, and clothes designers.

The countryside of France has a special magic as well: country villages with steep tiled roofs, set amid rolling hills; old castles and cobblestone streets; craggy cliffs overlooking the Mediterranean; rows and rows of grapevines disappearing into the distance; barrels filled with grapes; baskets containing bottles of locally made wine.

Sometimes it may seem like France is not one country, but many countries—each with a charm all its own.

INSIDE FRANCE

France covers 211,208 square miles, an area that's about four-fifths the size of Texas. Much of the country is bordered by mountains: the French Alps in the southeast; the Juras in the east, and the Vosges in the northeast. The Pyrenees line the southern border, next to Spain.

The island of Corsica—sometimes referred to as "a mountain in the sea"—is also part of France. Corsica is located about 100 miles southeast of France, in the Mediterranean Sea. In addition, France has nine overseas possessions, including French Guiana in South America and Guadeloupe in the West Indies.

There are four major rivers in France: the Seine, which empties into the English Channel; the Loire and the Garonne, which empty into the Bay of Biscay; and the Rhône, which empties into the Mediterranean Sea. In the center of France is the Massif Central, a plateau that makes up about 15 percent of France's total area. This area is often called the Central Highlands.

This is one of the many beautiful bridges that passes over the Seine River as it flows through Paris.

The beautiful château of Chenonceaux arches over the Cher River in the Loire Valley. During World War II, its unique position—half in the occupied territory and half in the free zone—allowed many refugees to flee from the Nazis.

The climate varies from region to region. In the western coastal area, winds from the Atlantic Ocean create a rainy climate with cool winters and mild summers. Along the Mediterranean coast, the summers are hot and dry and the winters mild with some rain. Inland, there is a sharper contrast between seasons.

Except for some periods during the 1800's, France has been a democracy since 1789. The president, elected by the people, appoints a prime minister, who in turn heads the council of ministers. The law-making parliament is divided into two departments: the National Assembly and the Senate.

Local government divisions, called communes, range from small villages to large cities. They are headed by a mayor and a council. Regional divisions are called metropolitan departments, and are run by locally elected council members as well as commissioners appointed by the national government.

SPECIAL EVENTS IN FRANCE

With a population that is mostly Roman Catholic, France celebrates many holidays that are connected with the church. Christmas Eve in Paris finds thousands of people flocking to the cathedral of Notre Dame for midnight mass. A number of cities hold a festival called *Carnaval* on the last day before Lent. In some rural areas, there is a bonfire celebration that combines John the Baptist Day with an ancient Celtic summer solstice observance.

Pardons are traditional religious celebrations that take place only in Brittany. Townspeople gather together to pay tribute to their local saint, to make vows, or to pray for forgiveness. Wearing elaborate costumes and holding candles or statues of saints, the people form a parade and march through the streets.

Costumes and revelry are very much a part of this Carnaval celebration in Nice.

A military parade winds through the streets of Paris on Bastille Day, France's national holiday.

Bastille Day, July 14, is France's national holiday. In 1789, during the French Revolution, the people of Paris overtook the fortified prison of Bastille, and that's where the holiday gets its name. Bastille Day in Paris includes a military parade, street dances, and fireworks.

One summer sporting event that attracts world-wide attention is the *Tour de France*. This is a three-week bicycle race that covers most of the country. The race finishes along the famed *Champs Elysées* in Paris, and draws thousands of spectators each year. It's been called the "World Series" of bicycle racing. Other famous sporting events are the Le Mans car race, a 24-hour endurance race through the streets of Le Mans, and the French Open tennis tournament.

The arts, too, have their share of festivities. The Cannes Film Festival is an international event for the movie business. Other notable events include the Nice Jazz Parade and the Avignon Drama Festival. And there's simply no end to the local concerts, ballets, operas, and art exhibits.

AGRICULTURE IN FRANCE

Shakespeare once poetically referred to France as "this best garden of the world, our fertile France." That phrase still applies today. Ninety percent of France's soil is fertile, and 60 percent of the land is used for agriculture. In fact, France is the largest food producer and exporter in all of Western Europe.

The soil is richest in the north and east. Crops here include wheat, sugarbeets, potatoes, and vegetables such as beans, carrots, cauliflower, and tomatoes. Grapes, used for making wine, grow well in the drier climate of southern France. Apple orchards and herds of sheep and cattle dot the grassy countryside in northwestern France. Fishing fleets off the coasts of Brittany and Normandy bring in cod, monkfish, oysters, and many other varieties of seafood.

Geese are raised on special farms in some areas of France. Fatted goose liver is a French delicacy.

A good variety of fruit is offered for sale in this outdoor market in Paris.

Since World War II, agricultural practices throughout much of the world have become more technical and efficient. This has changed the nature of farming in France, as in other developed countries. Gone are the days when French farmers were likely to be poor, illiterate peasants. Many farmers today are quite prosperous, and the cooperatives they've formed are very powerful politically.

Before 1945, more than 35 percent of the French population was involved in farming. In the years that followed, more and more people left the farms and moved to the cities, where new industries were springing up. Today, farmers make up just seven percent of the country's population.

Food processing is an important industry in France—as one would expect in a country that produces so much food. Bread, meats, butter, and fruit preserves are some examples. The most important products, however, are wine and cheese. France produces thousands of different wines, and more than 400 kinds of cheese!

WINE IN FRANCE

Wine plays a large role in the daily life of the French people. It is usually served with lunch and dinner, in restaurants as well as in private homes. Formal meals may include three or four different wines, each one matched to the course being served. What else would one expect? After all, with the exception of Italy, France produces more wine than any other country. The province of Burgundy alone produces more than 40 million bottles of wine each year!

But France is not famous just for the quantity of its wines. Quality counts too, and the French have taken great care to ensure the fine reputation of their wines. In 1935, France passed detailed laws to regulate wine production. As a result, wines are put into categories according to region, alcoholic content, and the method of production.

France is the world's second-largest producer of wine. These vineyards are found at Carcassonne, one of the few walled cities remaining in the world.

A winemaker in Côte d'Or stands proudly before his barrels of wine. Côte d'Or, a region in Burgundy, is known for producing some of the world's finest wines.

The type and quality of wine depends on a number of factors, including climate and the variety of grapes used. Soil is especially important. If the same variety of grapes is grown in different regions with similar climates, the resulting wines will be very different! That's why the name of the region the grapes come from is so important in identifying the wine.

The Provence region is famous for its rosés, Burgundy for its red wines, and the Loire Valley for its white wines. Other regions associated with wine making are Alsace, Bordeaux, Cognac, and, of course, Champagne. Incidentally, most Americans have never had "real" champagne. According to French law, the name applies only to champagne produced in a certain way in the province of Champagne.

While the best French wines can be very expensive, there are all sorts of very good wines available at reasonable prices. Sometimes the most enjoyable wines come from small, rural winemakers. These winemakers may store their wines in caves and offer "tastings" to visitors.

FOOD CUSTOMS IN FRANCE

Perhaps more than any other nationality, the French are noted for their devotion to good food. A well-prepared meal, served in an unhurried atmosphere and shared with family or friends, is considered one of life's greatest pleasures.

There are several styles of cooking in France. *Haute cuisine*—gourmet cooking—is what people are usually referring to when they make comments about the richness of French food. This style of cooking uses a lot of butter, cream, eggs, and expensive ingredients. Much care is taken to serve the meal as artfully as possible. The tradition began in the late 1700's with the elaborate 12-hour feasts of King Louis XIV.

Fresh bread is an essential part of a good French meal. Even the pigeons agree!

A merchant peddles vegetables to a restaurant chef at an open market in Cahors.

In *la nouvelle cuisine française* ("the new French cooking"), the emphasis is on fresh, light ingredients that are cooked quickly to bring out flavor. *Cuisine bourgeoise* is high-quality home cooking. Specialties vary from region to region, but using fresh ingredients is always important. Many families shop for food nearly every day, either in busy open markets or in specialty shops.

Breakfast in France is likely to be simple—bread or *croissants* served with butter and jam, and strong coffee or tea. Lunch is the main meal of the day throughout much of France, with many shops and businesses closing between noon and two. Dinner is usually served late, around eight o'clock.

In a typical French meal, the food is served one course at a time. Normally the meal begins with an *hors d'oeuvre*, soup, or both. The main course, usually meat and a vegetable, comes next, followed by a green salad. Next comes a serving of cheese. And finally—dessert! Fresh fruit is often served, but there are plenty of other choices as well, such as pastries, fruit tarts, and *crêpes* with whipped cream. Bread is always on the table. Wine, or perhaps beer or mineral water, accompanies the meal.

REGIONAL COOKING IN FRANCE

In a land as varied as France, it comes as no surprise that the food, too, often differs from place to place. Some of these differences are influenced mainly by geography—seafood specialties in the coastal areas of Brittany or Provence, for example, or cheeses made from goat's milk in the mountainous areas of southeastern France.

Other regional differences are influenced by the culture of nearby countries, and vice versa. The cooks in southwestern France often use sausages, peppers, and tomatoes, just as in Spain. And the foods of Alsace and Lorraine in northeastern France are similar to those in nearby Germany. The best-known dish from this region, *quiche lorraine*, consists of eggs, cream, and bacon in a pastry shell.

Omelettes were invented on the island of Mont-Saint-Michel. It's only an island at high tide!

Foie gras—fatted goose liver—is often used to make a rich and delicate pâté.

Crêpes—thin pancakes made of egg, flour, and milk—are a tradition in Brittany. They can be filled with meat, vegetables, or fruit. Crêpes are popular throughout France, but especially in Brittany, where there are more than 1800 crêperies!

From Provence comes *bouillabaisse*, a saffron-flavored seafood stew; and *ratatouille*, a rich vegetable dish of eggplant, zucchini, and tomatoes. From southwestern France comes the hearty *cassoulet*, a stew of white beans, sausage, pork, mutton, and goose. The world-famous *omelette* was developed in Normandy, on the coastal island of Mont-Saint-Michel. Various types of *pâtés*—chopped, spiced meat—are found throughout the country, perhaps the most elegant being *foie gras*. This pâté is made from the liver of fatted geese or ducks. There is almost no limit to French specialties, many of which are popular in other countries as well.

19

A FESTIVE MEAL

French Onion Soup
Green Salad (see page 27)
Tournedos of Beef
Roasted Potatoes
Chocolate Mouse
Fresh Fruit and Cheese

A festive meal in France is meant to take a long time. Each course is served separately, usually with time for conversation between each one. An exception would be vegetables or potatoes, which are served with the main course. (In this meal, the roasted potatoes should be served with the tournedos.)

French Onion Soup

> 2 tablespoons butter
> 4 medium onions, sliced thinly
> salt and pepper to taste
> 1 ½ tablespoons "all-purpose" flour
> 3 10 ½-ounce cans beef broth
> 2 ½ cans water
> ½ cup white wine
> stale or toasted French bread, sliced ½ inch thick
> 12 ounces grated Swiss cheese

1. Melt the butter in a large saucepan (5 or more quarts). Add the sliced onions and cook on medium heat until they are dark brown, around 30 minutes. Stir frequently so the onions do not burn.
2. Stir in the flour and cook until flour is brown. While stirring, slowly add beef broth, wine, and water. Bring to a boil. Reduce heat and simmer for 1 hour or longer. Skim off foam from the top with a spoon.
3. Put the soup in ovenproof bowls. Place a slice of bread on top and cover with cheese. Place the bowls on a cookie sheet and set the oven to broil. Broil about 5 minutes, just until cheese is melted and lightly browned. Serves 6.

**Tournedos of Beef
with Béarnaise Sauce**

Tournedos of Beef with Béarnaise Sauce

> *3 tablespoons butter*
> *4 shallots, finely chopped*
> *¹/₂ pound mushrooms, finely chopped*
> *salt and pepper, to taste*
> *4 teaspoons tomato paste*
> *1–2 tablespoons olive oil*
> *6 beef filets mignons, or other tender beef steaks*

1. Heat the butter in a small frying pan on medium heat. Add the shallots and sauté until soft, 4–5 minutes. Add the mushrooms and cook 10 minutes more, stirring frequently. Remove from heat. Stir in salt, pepper, and tomato paste.
2. Make the béarnaise sauce (see recipe next page). Put on top of a pan of medium-hot water to keep warm while you finish preparing the meal.
3. Heat the oil on medium high heat in a large frying pan. Cook the steaks 2–4 minutes each side, depending on how you like them done.
4. Serve on warm plates and top with mushrooms and béarnaise sauce. Serves 6.

Béarnaise Sauce

1 shallot, finely chopped
1 teaspoon tarragon
1/8 teaspoon freshly ground pepper
1 tablespoon wine vinegar
1 tablespoon white wine, or white cooking wine
1 tablespoon water
1 egg yolk
6 tablespoons butter, melted
1/8 teaspoon salt

1. In a small saucepan, combine shallots, tarragon, pepper, vinegar, and wine. Cook on high heat until 1 teaspoon of liquid remains. Remove from heat.
2. Over medium heat, add the water and egg yolk to the saucepan, stirring constantly with a whisk. As soon as the sauce thickens (2–3 minutes), remove from heat. Continue using the whisk for 30 seconds. If you cook it too much, the egg will look like a scrambled egg and the sauce will be ruined. However, the sauce should be thick enough to stick to the whisk.
3. Let the sauce cool for 2 minutes. Slowly add the melted butter, a little at a time, stirring constantly with the whisk. (The butter must not be hotter than the mixture.)
4. Whisk in the salt. To keep the sauce warm, set the pan in another pan half full of medium-hot water. The sauce can't be reheated, so don't let it cool.

Roasted Potatoes

6 tablespoons butter
15–20 small potatoes (or 4–5 large potatoes,
   quartered), peeled
salt and pepper to taste

1. Preheat oven to 475°.
2. Melt the butter in a large cast-iron fry pan on top of the stove.
3. Add the potatoes a few at a time, coating them thoroughly with butter.

4. Place the pan in the oven. Shake the pan every 10 minutes and/or turn the potatoes by using a large spoon so they brown evenly on all sides. Bake about 1 hour.
5. Remove from pan when finished, place in serving bowl, and sprinkle with salt and pepper. Serves 6.

Roasted Potatoes

Chocolate Mousse

1/2 cup semisweet chocolate chips
4 tablespoons unsalted butter
4 eggs, yolks and whites separated
1/8 teaspoon cream of tartar

1. Put the chocolate chips and the butter in a heavy saucepan. Melt over low heat, stirring until smooth. Remove from heat. Using a whisk, stir in the egg yolks.
2. In a large bowl, beat the egg whites and cream of tartar with an electric beater until stiff peaks can be made.
3. With the whisk, mix about 1/3 of the egg whites into the chocolate mixture. Then, using a rubber spatula, stir in the rest of the egg whites until smooth.
4. Put into 6 wine glasses or bowls and refrigerate 2 or more hours. Serve cold. Serves 6.

LUNCH IN BRITTANY

Seafood Crêpes with Mornay Sauce
Crudités (assorted raw vegetables)
French Bread

These crêpes are filled with scallops, but you could also use crabmeat, shrimp, or lobster.

Seafood Crêpes

2 tablespoons butter
¹/₄ cup finely chopped onion
1 garlic clove, minced
1 pound scallops, drained and set on a paper towel
¹/₂ cup Swiss cheese, grated
1 cup Mornay sauce (see recipe next page)
4 6-inch crêpes (see recipe next page)

1. Sauté onions and garlic in butter until soft. Add scallops and sauté for about 15 minutes. Drain. Add just enough Mornay sauce to coat the scallops well.
2. Spoon ¼ of the scallops across the middle of a crêpe. Fold the sides of the crêpe over the scallops, then turn crêpe over onto an oven-proof platter. Repeat with other 3 crêpes.
3. Pour the remaining Mornay sauce over the crêpes. Sprinkle the grated Swiss cheese on top. Broil for about 5 minutes, or until the Mornay sauce starts to get brown. Serves 4.

Crêpes

> 2 eggs
> 1 cup milk
> 2/3 cup white flour
> salt and pepper to taste
> 2 tablespoons melted butter or margarine

1. Using a whisk, stir together the eggs, flour, and half of the milk until smooth. Stir in the rest of the milk and let batter sit for 15 or 20 minutes.
2. Just before making the crêpes, stir in the melted butter.
3. Heat a 6- or 7-inch crêpe pan over medium-high heat. Pour about 2 tablespoons of batter in the pan and quickly swirl pan so batter covers the bottom. As soon as batter looks dry, turn crêpe. Cook about 15 seconds on the other side, and remove.
4. Stack crêpes as you cook them. This recipe will make about 12 crêpes. (Those you don't use may be refrigerated or frozen.)

Mornay Sauce

> 1 1/2 tablespoons butter
> 1 1/2 tablespoons flour
> 1 cup milk
> pinch of salt
> 1/8 teaspoon pepper
> nutmeg to taste
> 1/3 cup grated Swiss cheese

1. Melt butter in small saucepan, then add flour and stir until the mixture is creamy.
2. Gradually add the milk while stirring. In 2–3 minutes the sauce will thicken and start to boil. Remove from heat and add seasonings and cheese. Return to burner and stir while bringing to a boil. Set aside. If too thick, the sauce may be thinned with milk. Makes about 1 cup of sauce.

BRUNCH IN LORRAINE

Quiche Lorraine
Green Salad with Classic French Dressing
Croissants

Quiche, a type of egg pie, was invented in the province of Lorraine, an area in northeastern France. The salad can be served as a separate course, or with the quiche. Serve the croissants with butter and jam.

Quiche Lorraine

> 1 9-inch deep dish pie shell
> 1 egg white, beaten
> 6 strips of bacon, cooked crisp
> 2 cups milk or cream
> 3 eggs
> $1/4$ teaspoon salt
> $1/8$ teaspoon pepper
> 1–2 teaspoons Dijon mustard
> $1/8$ teaspoon nutmeg
> 1 teaspoon chopped chives or minced onion
> 1 cup Swiss cheese, diced

1. Brush the pie shell with egg white and prick it well with a fork.
2. Cook the bacon until almost crisp. Drain on paper towels. Cool. Crumble into pie shell.
3. Beat the eggs. Add milk, salt, pepper, mustard, nutmeg, and chives or onion. Mix well.
4. Place diced cheese in the bottom of the pie shell.
5. Pour egg mixture into shell. Bake about 45 minutes at 375° or until top is golden brown. To test for doneness, insert a knife in the center. The knife will come out clean if the quiche is done. Serves 4.

Quiche Lorraine

Green Salad

> 1 small head Bibb or Boston lettuce
> 1 small head romaine or iceberg lettuce
> 1/4 cup grated Parmesan cheese
> 1 avocado, sliced
> 4 cherry tomatoes

1. Wash and drain salad greens. Cover and refrigerate for at least half an hour.
2. Tear the lettuce into small pieces. Add the Parmesan cheese and about 1/2 cup of the dressing. Toss well. Put on salad plates and garnish each with avocado slices and a tomato. Serves 4.

Classic French Dressing

> 2 tablespoons lemon juice
> 2 tablespoons wine vinegar
> 1 garlic clove, cut in half
> 1 teaspoon Dijon mustard
> 1/2 teaspoon salt
> 1/2 teaspoon pepper
> 3/4 cup olive oil or light vegetable oil

1. Put all ingredients into a pint jar. Cover jar tightly and shake well. Shake again just before serving. Makes 1 cup of dressing.

27

AN EVERYDAY MEAL

Cheese Omelette
Fresh Fruit
French Bread

Omelettes can be filled with almost anything, but this one uses Swiss cheese. Slices of fresh fruit and French bread round out the meal.

**Cheese
Omelette**

Cheese Omelette

>   *2–3 eggs*
>   *1 teaspoon chopped fresh parsley*
>   *1 teaspoon chopped fresh chives*
>   *salt and pepper to taste*
>   *2 teaspoons butter*
>   *1/3 cup grated Swiss cheese*

1. Beat the eggs and spices in a bowl until blended.
2. Melt butter over medium-high heat in a non-stick pan, then pour in the eggs. Stir eggs with spoon, just until they start to set.
3. Lay cheese across middle of omelette. After about 1 minute, fold the 2 sides over the cheese with a spatula. Slide the omelette out of the pan so it turns over on the plate. Keep omelette warm in oven if you need to make more. Serves 1.

GLOSSARY OF COOKING TERMS

For those readers who are less experienced in the kitchen, the following list explains the cooking terms used in this book.

Chopped	Cut into small pieces measuring about ½ inch thick. Finely chopped pieces should be about ⅛ inch thick.
Diced	Cut into small cubes.
Garnished	Decorated.
Grated	Cut into small pieces by using a grater.
Greased	Having been lightly coated with oil, butter, or margarine to prevent sticking.
Knead	To work dough with one's hands.
Marinate	To cover and soak with a mixture of juices, called a marinade.
Minced	Chopped into very tiny pieces.
Pinch	The amount you can pick up between your thumb and forefinger.
Reserve	To set aside an ingredient for future use.
Sauté	To cook food in oil, butter, or margarine at high temperature, while stirring constantly.
Shredded	Cut into lengths of 1–2 inches, about ¼ inch across. Finely shredded ingredients should be about ⅛ inch across.
Simmer	To cook on a stove at the lowest setting.
Sliced	Cut into thin slices that show the original shape of the object.
Toss	To mix the ingredients in a salad.
Whisk	To beat using a hand whisk or electric mixer.

FRENCH COOKING

To make the recipes in this book, you will need the following equipment and ingredients, which may not be in your kitchen:

Beef broth While you can make your own "from scratch," it is easier to buy a can in the soup section of a supermarket.

Dijon mustard This is a French-style mustard that is darker in color than the common yellow mustard. It has little bits of mustard seed in it.

Fresh produce Most supermarkets will have eggplant, zucchini, summer squash, green peppers, and avocados all year round. Bibb, Boston, and romaine lettuce are of the "leafy" type and may be a little harder to find, but most markets will have at least one of them on hand. Iceberg lettuce is the common "head" lettuce. Shallots are sort of a cross between garlic and onions—they'll usually be next to the fresh garlic in the produce section.

Garlic Fresh garlic can be found in the produce section of supermarkets. Each bulb can be broken into sections called cloves. You have to remove the brittle skin around each clove before chopping it.

Herbs If possible, it's best to buy fresh chives, thyme, parsley, bay leaves, basil, oregano, and tarragon from a farmer's market or the produce section of a supermarket. If these aren't available, use dried herbs, which are in the spice section.

Olive oil A cooking oil made by pressing olives, available in most supermarkets.

Spices Nutmeg and cream of tartar will be found in the spice section of a supermarket. You can sometimes find fresh nutmeg (it looks like a nut) in the produce section and grate your own.

Sausages of all kinds are a popular food in southwestern France.

INDEX

We would like to thank and acknowledge the following people for the use of their photographs and transparencies:

Mark E. Ahlstrom: cover, cover inset, 8, 9, 21, 23, 24, 27, 28; French Government Tourist Office: 2, 7, 10, 11, 12, 13, 14, 15, 16, 17, 18, 19, 30

Produced by Mark E. Ahlstrom (The Bookworks)
Typesetting and layout by The Final Word
Photo research by Judith Ahlstrom